BE YOU

A *52-week* self-care journal *for* slowing down *and* reconnecting *with* your goals

Amy Knapp

INTRODUCTION

Be bold. Be happy. Be *you*.

Tap into your inner self and explore who you truly are: your dreams, your creativity, and your goals. This journal is meant to inspire you and help you discover different things about yourself that you might not have known. With a prompt for each week, this journal will guide you through a year of fun and uncomplicated self-reflections to remind you to always be *you*.

• THIS MONTH •

BE AUTHENTIC

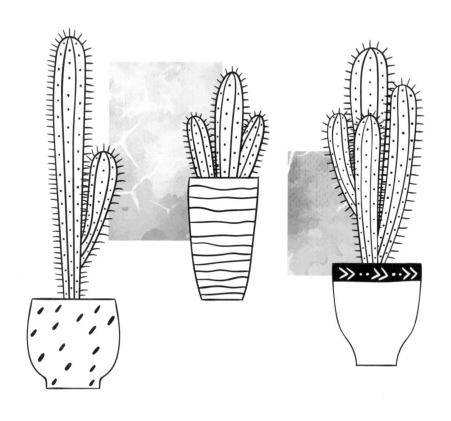

**SURROUND YOURSELF
WITH PEOPLE WHO
GET YOU.**

Week 1

What is
your favorite
version of you?

LOVE YOURSELF,
EMBRACE YOUR FLAWS,
AND NEVER LET
THE OPINION OF
OTHERS AFFECT YOUR
SELF-CONFIDENCE.
YOU ARE ENOUGH.

• BETHANY MOTA •

1.

2.

3.

4.

5.

Write twelve words that best describe you.

6.

7.

8.

9.

10.

11.

12.

Week 2

Who loves you for who you are now,
not who you might become?

He said, "You are beautiful."
I told him, "Beautiful is a lazy
and lousy way to describe me."

• IJEOMA UMEBINYUO •

List ways you can show your
thankfulness for these people.

Week 3

What imperfections do you love
the most about yourself?

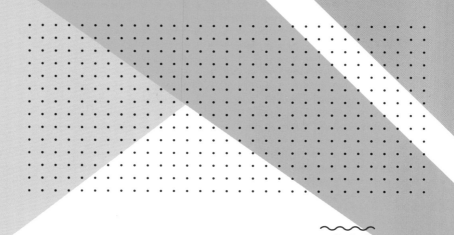

YOU ARE MAGNIFICENT BEYOND MEASURE, PERFECT IN YOUR IMPERFECTIONS, AND WONDERFULLY MADE.

• ABIOLA ABRAMS •

NO MATTER WHO YOU ARE,
NO MATTER WHERE
YOU COME FROM,
YOU ARE BEAUTIFUL.

• MICHELLE OBAMA •

Write seven words
describing who
you want to be.

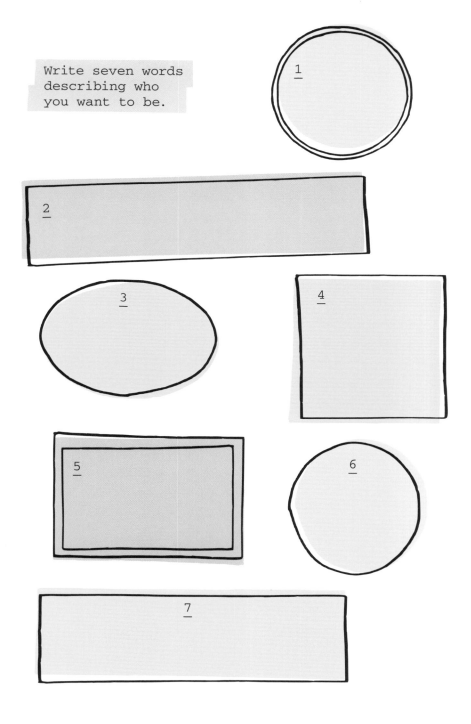

1

2

3

4

5

6

7

Week 4

List five great things about yourself.

1

2

3

4

5

Pick five words that will **not** define you!

1

2

3

4

5

List five fantastic
things about your
best friends.

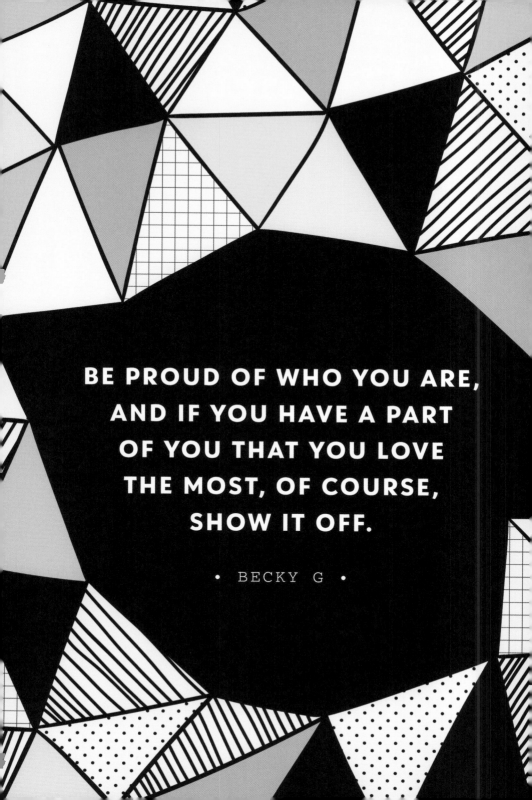

BE PROUD OF WHO YOU ARE,
AND IF YOU HAVE A PART
OF YOU THAT YOU LOVE
THE MOST, OF COURSE,
SHOW IT OFF.

• BECKY G •

• THIS MONTH •

BE
ADVENTUROUS

Week 1

If you could live anywhere, where would it be?
Why?

**IF WE WERE MEANT TO
STAY IN ONE PLACE,
WE WOULD HAVE ROOTS
INSTEAD OF FEET.**

• RACHEL WOLCHIN •

Mark five places
you want to see
in your lifetime.

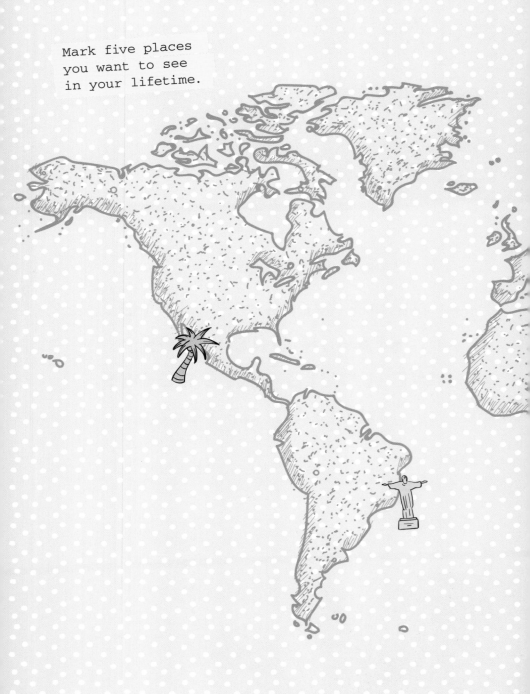

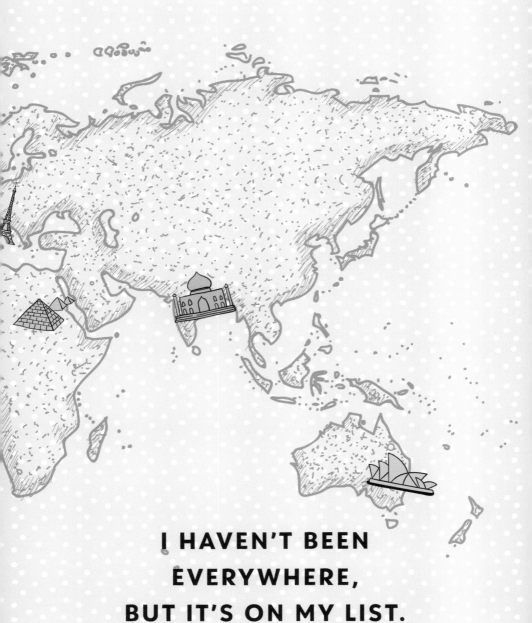

I HAVEN'T BEEN EVERYWHERE, BUT IT'S ON MY LIST.

· SUSAN SONTAG ·

Week 2

What has been your greatest adventure?

What do you wish for your next trip?

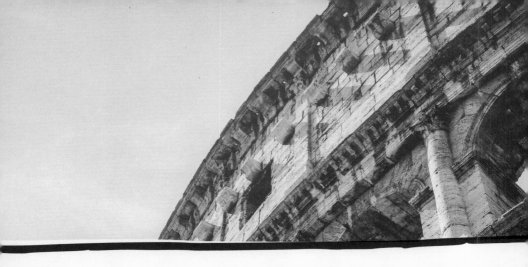

I AM NOT THE SAME HAVING SEEN THE MOON SHINE ON THE OTHER SIDE OF THE WORLD.

• MARY ANNE RADMACHER •

Week 3

List as many things you can think of that you could do **now** that you've never done before.

Week 4

Who would you take on a road trip across the country? Why?

**PEOPLE DON'T
TAKE TRIPS.
TRIPS TAKE PEOPLE.**

• JOHN STEINBECK •

• THIS MONTH •

BE
THOUGHTFUL

Week 1

What impact would you like to leave
on the world?

LET US MAKE OUR FUTURE NOW, AND LET US MAKE OUR DREAMS TOMORROW'S REALITY.

• MALALA YOUSAFZAI •

Week 2

What three things were you scared to try but ended up loving?

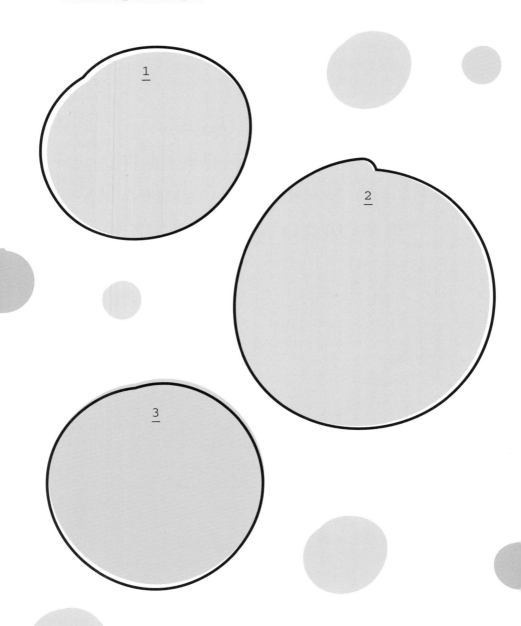

1

2

3

EVERYTHING YOU'VE EVER WANTED IS ON THE OTHER SIDE OF FEAR.

• GEORGE ADDAIR •

What are you scared of? What can you do to
overcome your fears more and more each day?

**DON'T LET THE FEAR OF
WHAT *COULD* HAPPEN MAKE
NOTHING HAPPEN.**

Week 3

What do you wish you had tried in the past but didn't?
Can you recreate it and try now?

I DWELL IN POSSIBILITY.

• EMILY DICKINSON •

Week 4

Have you ever believed something about yourself and proven it untrue? What was it?

WHAT LIES BEHIND YOU AND WHAT LIES IN FRONT OF YOU PALES IN COMPARISON TO WHAT LIES INSIDE OF YOU.

• RALPH WALDO EMERSON •

FIND OUT WHO
YOU ARE AND BE
THAT PERSON. THAT'S
WHAT YOUR SOUL
WAS PUT ON THIS
EARTH TO BE.
FIND THAT TRUTH,
LIVE THAT TRUTH,
AND EVERYTHING
ELSE WILL COME.

• ELLEN DEGENERES •

Break more boundaries.
What rules can you explore and break?

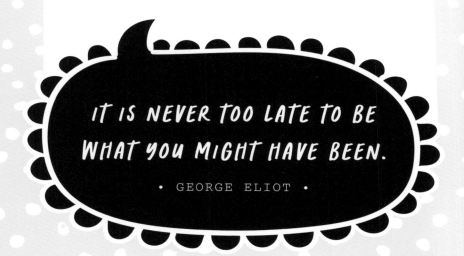

IT IS NEVER TOO LATE TO BE
WHAT YOU MIGHT HAVE BEEN.

• GEORGE ELIOT •

• THIS MONTH •

BE HAPPY

Week 1

How do you measure happiness?
Jot down your favorite things to do when you
need a pick-me-up.

LIFE IS BETTER WHEN
YOU'RE LAUGHING!

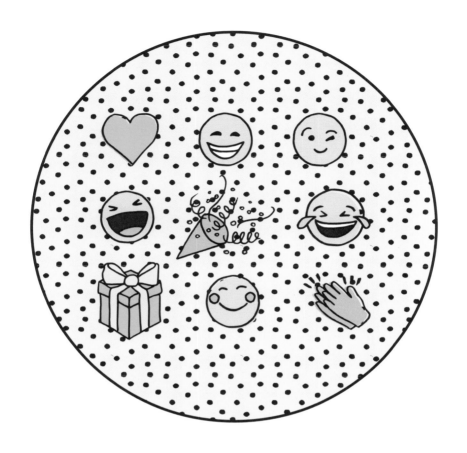

DO WHAT MAKES YOU HAPPY WITHIN THE CONFINES OF THE LEGAL SYSTEM.

• ELLEN DEGENERES •

Week 2

Who is the one person who can *always* bring a smile to your face?
How does he or she do it?

A SMILE IS A CURVE THAT
SETS EVERYTHING STRAIGHT.

• PHYLLIS DILLER •

Week 3

What are some of your superpowers you use to make others happy?

WHOEVER IS HAPPY
WILL MAKE OTHERS HAPPY TOO.

• ANNE FRANK •

Week 4

What is your favorite childhood memory?

HAPPY TIMES COME AND GO—BUT THE MEMORIES STAY FOREVER.

Write about five recent moments that made you happy. Moments both big and small are capable of creating joy!

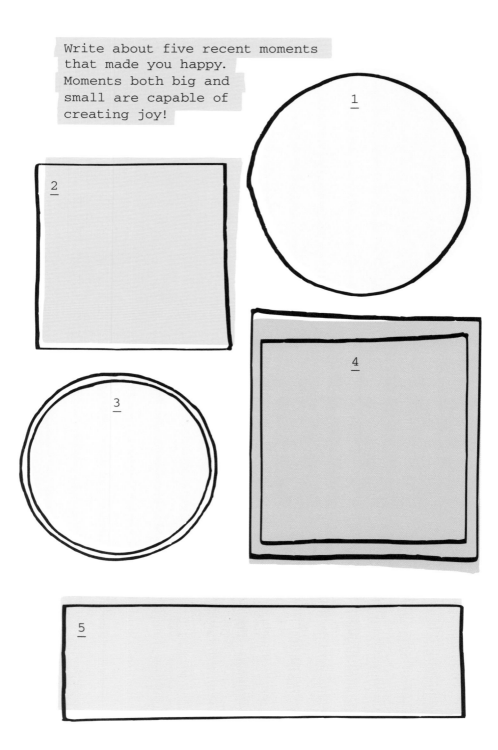

1

2

3

4

5

THERE ARE SO MANY BEAUTIFUL REASONS TO BE HAPPY.

• THIS MONTH •

BE CREATIVE

Week 1

EVERYTHING I LEARNED, I LEARNED FROM THE MOVIES.

· AUDREY HEPBURN ·

Would your movie be a romantic comedy or a drama or something else altogether?

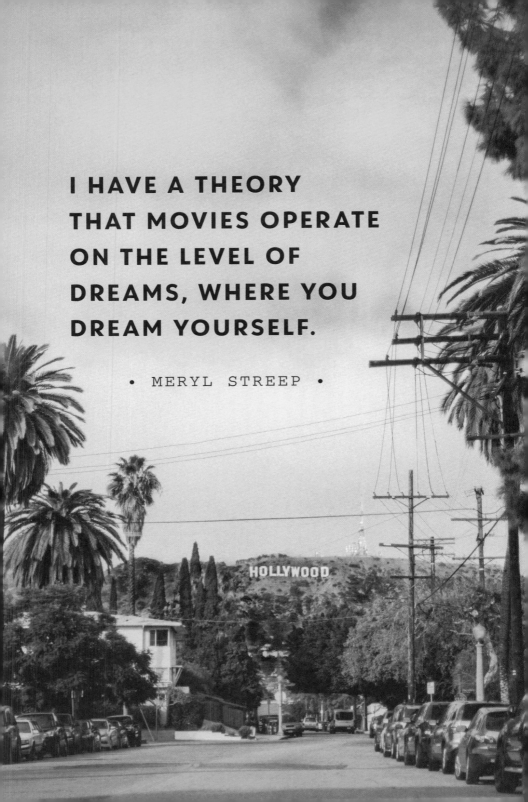

I HAVE A THEORY
THAT MOVIES OPERATE
ON THE LEVEL OF
DREAMS, WHERE YOU
DREAM YOURSELF.

• MERYL STREEP •

Week 2

What would the title of a book about you be called?

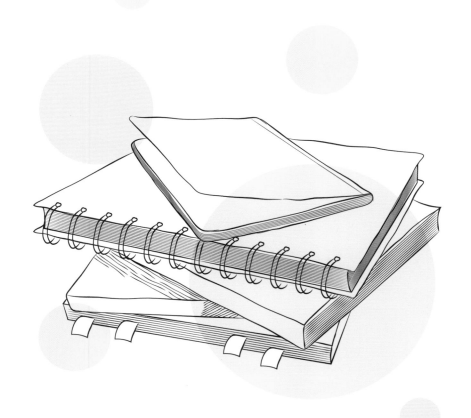

IF THERE'S A BOOK THAT YOU WANT TO READ, BUT IT HASN'T BEEN WRITTEN YET, THEN YOU MUST WRITE IT.

• TONI MORRISON •

What is the plot of your book? Biggest arc?
Message you hope readers take away?

Week 3

Write an acrostic poem using your name.
What do these words say about you?

DELIGHTFUL

FIERCE

BEAUTIFUL

MAGICAL

Week 4

Draw a self-portrait.

MY AWESOME PORTRAIT

What words speak to who you are? What do you see in your self-portrait that you wish others would see?

CREATIVITY IS THE WAY
I SHARE MY SOUL
WITH THE WORLD.

• BRENÉ BROWN •

• THIS MONTH •

BE EMPOWERED

Week 1

What goals do you have for this month?
This year?
Throughout your life?

MONTHLY GOALS	YEARLY GOALS

LIFE GOALS

WHATEVER
YOU'RE THINKING,
THINK BIGGER.

OUT-DREAM YOURSELF.

Week 2

What has been your biggest accomplishment to date?

I DIDN'T COME THIS FAR
TO ONLY COME THIS FAR.

• UNKNOWN •

Week 3

What are three big dreams you hope
to accomplish?

1

2

3

**YOUR POTENTIAL
IS ENDLESS.**

What needs to happen in your life to
achieve your dreams?

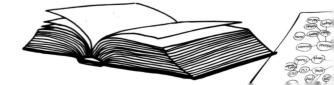

Week 4

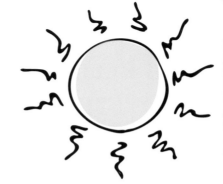

What gets you out of bed
and motivated each day?

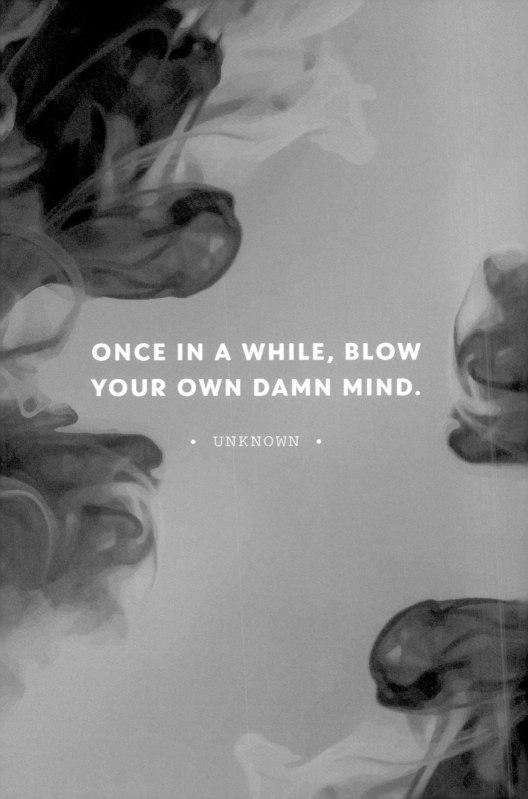

ONCE IN A WHILE, BLOW
YOUR OWN DAMN MIND.

• UNKNOWN •

• THIS MONTH •

BE HONEST

Week 1

Write a letter to your future self about
lessons you have learned.
How did you get here?

**ALWAYS REMEMBER:
BE KIND, BE FAIR,
BE HONEST, BE TRUE,
AND ALL OF THESE THINGS
WILL COME BACK TO YOU.**

What is something you want **you** to remember about who you are today?

Week 2

What is the wisest thing you've ever been told?
How did this shape your life?

ALWAYS SPEAK THE TRUTH, EVEN IF YOUR VOICE SHAKES.

Week 3

What scares you most? Why?

LET YOUR SMILE CHANGE
THE WORLD, BUT DON'T LET
THE WORLD CHANGE
YOUR SMILE.

When do you feel most alive?

Does conquering your fears or proving them
wrong come into play in those moments?

Week 4

What's working in your life right now?
What needs a little more attention?

KILLING IT!

NEEDS WORK...

• THIS MONTH •

BE STRONG

Week 1

What was the toughest thing you've ever done?

LIFE IS TOUGH, MY DARLING,
BUT SO ARE YOU.

• STEPHANIE BENNETT-HENRY •

How does that define who you are today?

**IN DIVERSITY,
THERE IS BEAUTY AND
THERE IS STRENGTH.**

• MAYA ANGELOU •

IN THE END,
SOME OF YOUR GREATEST
PAINS BECOME YOUR
GREATEST STRENGTHS.

• DREW BARRYMORE •

Week 2

What failure in your life has given you the most perspective?

List three ways failure creates growth.
Now apply it to your own life.

Remind yourself why it is okay to fail.

Week 3

What are some of your obstacles right now?
What will it take to overcome them?

**THERE ARE NO REGRETS
IN LIFE. JUST LESSONS.**

· JENNIFER ANISTON ·

Week 4

How do you celebrate a win?

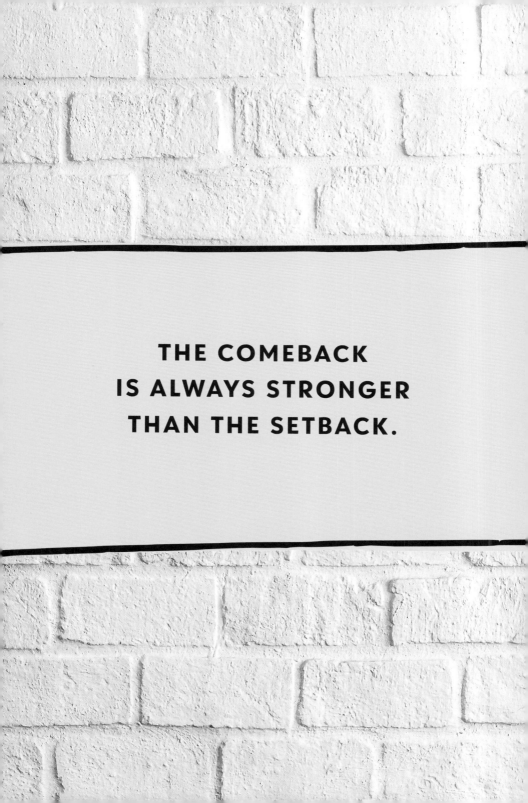

THE COMEBACK
IS ALWAYS STRONGER
THAN THE SETBACK.

In what ways are you stronger now than last year? Five years ago?

STORMS MAKE
TREES TAKE DEEPER
ROOTS.

BE SILLY

Week 1

How would you describe your sense of humor?

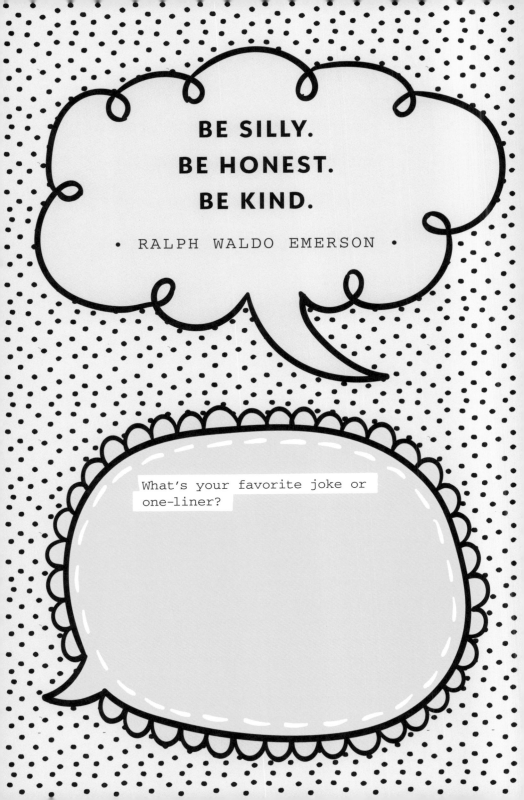

BE SILLY.
BE HONEST.
BE KIND.

· RALPH WALDO EMERSON ·

What's your favorite joke or one-liner?

Week 2

What are your favorite quirks about yourself?

Do you like to sing in the shower?
Eat ice cream for dinner?
What fun things make you *you*?

Week 3

What is something unexpected you could do **right now**? Go do it!
Write about how it felt when you did the unexpected.

**IF YOU CAN DANCE
AND BE FREE AND NOT
EMBARRASSED, YOU CAN
RULE THE WORLD.**

• AMY POEHLER •

What's your favorite song lyric, quote from a book, or line from a movie?

Week 4

If you could have any superpower in the
world, what would it be? Why?

• THIS MONTH •

BE THANKFUL

EXPECT NOTHING.
APPRECIATE EVERYTHING.

Week 1

What does it mean to be thankful?
List a few things you are thankful for.

Week 2

Write about a person you're thankful for.

When was the last time you told that person how much you appreciate him or her?

Week 3

What is a challenge you're facing right now?
How can you be thankful for it?

A GRATEFUL HEART
IS A MAGNET FOR
MIRACLES.

Week 4

How is your life different today from
one year ago?
What positive changes are you thankful for?

**GRATITUDE UNLOCKS
THE FULLNESS OF LIFE.**

• THIS MONTH •

BE HOPEFUL

Week 1

What does hope mean to you?

HOPE IS THE LITTLE VOICE YOU HEAR WHISPER "MAYBE" WHEN IT SEEMS THE ENTIRE WORLD IS SHOUTING "NO!"

• UNKNOWN •

**LEARN FROM YESTERDAY,
LIVE FOR TODAY,
HOPE FOR TOMORROW.**

• ALBERT EINSTEIN •

Week 2

What are your biggest dreams?

Have any of your dreams ever come true?
What were they?

ONCE YOU CHOOSE HOPE,

ANYTHING IS POSSIBLE.

WE ALL KEEP DREAMING, AND LUCKILY, DREAMS REALLY DO COME TRUE.

• KATIE HOLMES •

What do you think has made certain dreams
reality, and how can you realize more?

Week 3

What are six things you hope for other people in your life?

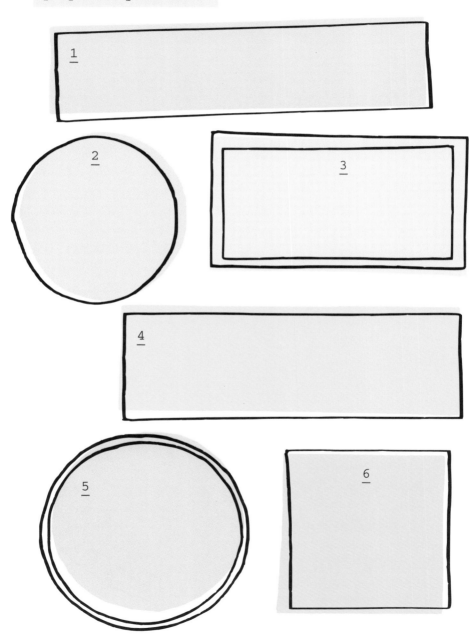

1

2

3

4

5

6

List a few ways you can help your hopes become realized.

WE HAVE THIS HOPE
AS AN ANCHOR
FOR THE SOUL.

• HEBREWS 6:19 •

Week 4

What would your life be like without hope?

**HOPE IS
THE ONLY THING
STRONGER THAN FEAR.**

Where can you infuse more hope into your life?

NOTHING CAN BE DONE
WITHOUT HOPE
AND CONFIDENCE.

• HELEN KELLER •

• THIS MONTH •

BE GIVING

Week 1

List some of the most important people in your life, along with a few reasons why you love them.

What are some common themes in those few
standout people?
How do you feel most loved by them?

THERE ARE SOME PEOPLE IN LIFE
THAT MAKE YOU LAUGH A LITTLE
LOUDER, SMILE A LITTLE BIGGER,
AND LIVE A LITTLE BETTER.

Week 2

How do you show others you love them?

IF YOU HAVE ONLY
ONE SMILE IN YOU,
GIVE IT TO THE PEOPLE
YOU LOVE.

· MAYA ANGELOU ·

List people in your life you could shower more love on.

I FEEL THAT THERE IS
NOTHING MORE TRULY ARTISTIC
THAN TO LOVE PEOPLE.

• VINCENT VAN GOGH •

Week 3

> **TO FALL IN LOVE WITH YOURSELF IS THE FIRST SECRET TO HAPPINESS.**
>
> • ROBERT MORLEY •

What do you love most about your life?

Week 4

What type of love is most important to you?
How do you define love and see it in
your life?